APPLE VISION PRO VR HEADSET MANUAL

Beyond Reality, Your Step By Step Guide To Apple Vision Pro

Desmond O. Allen

Book Copyright Notice.

Table of Contents

Chapter 1

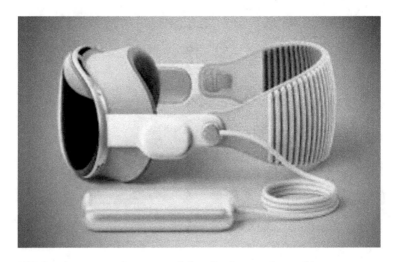

Welcome to the world of virtual reality

1.1 Overview of Apple's Vision Pro VR Headset
In an era characterized by technological marvels,
Apple once again takes center stage with the
introduction of the Vision Pro VR Headset. This

cutting-edge device represents the epitome of Apple's commitment to seamlessly integrating innovation into our daily lives. The Vision Pro isn't merely a piece of hardware; it's a testament to the convergence of design excellence, ergonomic precision, and technological sophistication.

1.1.1 Design Elegance:
The Vision Pro's design is a symphony of form and function, exemplifying Apple's design philosophy. Crafted from high-quality materials, its sleek and lightweight build is not only aesthetically pleasing but also optimized for comfort during extended use. The user-centric design ensures that the headset is not just a device but an extension of the user's experience.

1.1.2 Technological Advancements:

At the heart of the Vision Pro is a fusion of state-of-the-art hardware and software. The integration of advanced sensors, high-resolution displays, and powerful processors creates an immersive environment that transcends the boundaries of conventional reality. Apple's relentless pursuit of technological excellence is evident in every aspect of the headset's construction.

1.1.3 Seamless Integration:
The Vision Pro seamlessly integrates with other Apple devices, providing a holistic ecosystem that enhances the user experience. Whether it's interacting with your iPhone, iPad, or Mac, the Vision Pro becomes a versatile gateway, extending Apple's ecosystem into the realm of virtual reality. This integration not only amplifies the utility of the headset but also sets it apart in the VR landscape.

1.2 Evolution of Virtual Reality

To appreciate the Vision Pro fully, one must embark on a journey through the evolution of virtual reality. From its conceptual roots in science fiction to the clunky prototypes of the past, the trajectory of VR has been a fascinating narrative of innovation and progress. The Vision Pro stands at the pinnacle of this journey, encapsulating the culmination of breakthroughs that have defined the evolution of virtual reality.

1.2.1 Historical Milestones:

This section will explore key milestones in the evolution of virtual reality, starting from the first inklings of the concept to pivotal moments in hardware and software development. Understanding the challenges and triumphs along the way provides a context that enhances the user's appreciation for the Vision Pro as a product of continuous innovation.

1.2.2 Technological Transformations:
A detailed examination of the technological transformations within the VR landscape will shed light on the strides made in display technology, motion tracking, and user interface design. The Vision Pro, as a product of this technological evolution, becomes a culmination of years of experimentation, learning, and refinement.

1.2.3 User Experience Evolution:
Beyond the hardware, the evolution of VR extends to user experience. Examining how user interactions and interfaces have evolved over time helps users grasp the significance of the Vision Pro's user-friendly design and intuitive controls. This section will bridge the historical context with the

practical implications for users exploring the Vision Pro.

1.3 Purpose and Scope of the Manual

This manual transcends the traditional notion of instructional guides; it is a comprehensive companion crafted to empower users on their journey with the Apple Vision Pro VR Headset.

1.3.1 Empowering Users:

Users will find a detailed exploration of the Vision Pro, starting from the fundamental setup to the exploration of its most advanced features. The manual provides step-by-step guidance, ensuring users unlock the full potential of their VR experiences, catering to both beginners and seasoned enthusiasts.

1.3.2 Navigating Complexity:

Virtual reality can be intricate, and the Vision Pro is no exception. The manual simplifies this complexity, breaking down intricate features into digestible sections. Users, regardless of their familiarity with VR, will find clarity in navigating the intricacies of the headset, promoting a seamless and frustration-free experience.

1.3.3 Facilitating Exploration:
Beyond being an instructional guide, this manual serves as a tool for exploration. Users are encouraged to dive into a vast array of applications, customize their environments, and engage with the Vision Pro in ways that align with their unique interests and preferences. The manual fosters a sense of adventure, turning the Vision Pro into a canvas for personal expression within the virtual realm.

1.3.4 Fostering Community:
The Vision Pro experience extends beyond individual use. This manual aims to foster a sense of community by providing insights into upcoming developments, user recommendations, and a platform for users to share their experiences. The Vision Pro community becomes a collective of enthusiasts shaping the future of virtual reality, enriching the overall user experience.

As we embark on this multifaceted journey through the realms of virtual reality with the Apple Vision Pro VR Headset, let this manual be your comprehensive guide, enriching your understanding and empowering you to navigate the extraordinary possibilities that await beyond reality.

Chapter 2

Assembly and Unpacking

2.1 Contents of the Package
Opening the Apple Vision Pro VR Headset marks
the beginning of an adventure into the world of
augmented reality, not just an unboxing experience.
Apple's attention to detail in the box design is
indicative of their dedication to producing
high-quality products. When you open the lid,
you're met with an ensemble of thoughtfully placed

elements that form the core of your immersive experience.

2.1.1 The Apple Vision Pro VR Headset is the main draw.

The actual Vision Pro headset is tucked inside in the middle of the box. Its elegant lines and high-quality finish draw attention right away. From the movable head straps to the well-placed sensors, the careful engineering is evident. The headgear is the epitome of style and utility combined.

2.1.2 Essentials of Power and Connectivity

The necessary power and connectivity accessories are arranged around the headset. A variety of connectors, a charging cable, and a power converter guarantee that your Vision Pro is always prepared for use. Apple promises dependable and effective performance with these accessories, further demonstrating their commitment to a seamless user experience.

2.1.3 Documentation for Users

A carefully chosen collection of user manuals is located beneath the accessories. Apple makes sure users have access to all the information they need, from comprehensive manuals to fast start guides. The user-friendliness of the documentation is prioritized, including concise directions and helpful illustrations to ensure a seamless setup procedure.

2.1.4 Visual Appeal: Apple Logo and Add-ons

Apple's attention to detail is evident even in the package. The subtle integration of Apple branding fosters expectation and brand loyalty. To further improve the unboxing experience, concealed compartments may open to expose goodies like Apple stickers or other promotional materials.

2.2 Hardware Parts

To fully utilize the Vision Pro, it is essential to comprehend its hardware components. Every component contributes differently to the smooth and engrossing virtual reality experience.

2.2.1 Visibility and Materials

The Vision Pro's high-resolution display and cutting-edge optics are the foundation of its remarkable visual capabilities. The purpose of the lenses' engineering is to reduce distortion and improve clarity, giving users a realistic visual experience. This part will go into the technical details, describing how the optics and display combine to produce breathtaking images.

2.2.2 Components of Spatial Audio and Sound

Virtual reality's audio experience is a key component. Spatial audio technology is integrated into the Vision Pro, producing a three-dimensional auditory environment. This section will examine how Apple has made an immersive audio experience a top priority, from the integrated speakers to the audio processing capabilities.

2.2.3 Tracking Mechanisms and Sensors

The Vision Pro's flawless motion tracking is one of its main features. A number of carefully positioned sensors on the headgear enable this. This section will give a detailed look at how various sensors, such as accelerometers and gyroscopes, combine to convert movements in the actual world into the virtual environment.

2.2.4 Comfort and Construction Quality

The Vision Pro was designed with user comfort as the first priority. The ergonomic elements—such as the lightweight materials and adjustable head straps—will be discussed in this section. Comprehending the device's build quality not only improves comfort throughout extended use but also adds to its overall endurance and longevity.

2.3 First Steps in Setup
It's time to start the initial setup procedure now that the hardware has been examined and the components revealed. We take the necessary steps to make the Vision Pro a reality, and throughout, Apple's dedication to creating user-friendly experiences is evident.

2.3.1 Turning on for the initial instance
There is a sense of expectancy during the first power-up. In this section, users will learn how to

power on the Vision Pro for the first time, as well as explore the startup sequence and any preliminary calibration procedures.

2.3.2 Linking up with Apple Products

One of the main features of the Vision Pro experience is its seamless integration with other Apple products. The procedure for pairing the headset with iPhones, iPads, and Macs will be covered in this section. Beyond just connecting the dots, the integration forges a cohesive ecosystem that promotes a positive user experience.

2.3.3 Configuring Language and Region

A vital first step in making the Vision Pro experience uniquely yours is modifying the language and region settings. This section will walk users through the setup menu and make sure their preferences match their preferred language and location.

2.3.4 Creation of User Profiles

The Vision Pro gains a personal touch when a user profile is created. This section will go over how to create a user profile that suits your preferences, from avatars to customized settings. An immersive virtual reality world that is individualized can be accessed through the profile.

2.4 Linking to Equipment

Connecting to external devices is the next step after finishing the basic setup. This section will walk customers through the different connectivity choices available, whether it's syncing with a smartphone or connecting to a game console.

2.4.1 Internet Access via Wireless

When using suitable devices, wireless communication is supported by the Vision Pro. The procedures for setting up a wireless connection will be covered in this part, guaranteeing a cable-free experience without sacrificing excellent audio and video output.

2.4.2 Adapters and Wired Connections
The Vision Pro supports a variety of adapters to accommodate different devices for those who prefer a wired connection. With flexibility for many use cases, this section will walk customers through the process of connecting utilizing wired methods.

2.4.3 Troubleshooting and Compatibility Verification
For a flawless experience, compatibility with external devices must be guaranteed. A checklist to confirm compatibility and troubleshoot any

possible issues that can surface during the connecting procedure is provided in this section.

2.4.4 Updates for Software and Firmware

Firmware and software upgrades can be accessed through connecting to devices. The procedures for maintaining the most recent version of Vision Pro, which gives users access to the newest features, compatibility updates, and upgrades, are outlined in this section.

Users are now ready to dive into the amazing world of the Apple Vision Pro VR Headset after completing the packaging and setup process. The trip has only just begun; the next few chapters will reveal the plethora of opportunities and experiences that lie outside the realm of reality.

Chapter 3

Getting Started

It's a thrilling adventure to venture into the immersive world of the Apple Vision Pro VR Headset. This chapter walks you through all the important initial tasks, such as turning the device on, figuring out how to use the interface, comprehending simple motions and controls, and adjusting the straps to attain a comfortable fit.

3.1 Switches for On and Off

3.1.1 The Ritual of the Power Button

Learning how to use the power button on the Apple Vision Pro is the first step towards starting your virtual reality experience. This button, which is thoughtfully placed on the headset, starts a series of events that activate the gadget. To turn on the headset, press and hold; to turn it off politely, press and hold again. Knowing this procedure will guarantee that your virtual reality experiences begin and end well.

3.1.2 The Initial Order

Upon turning on the Vision Pro, an enthralling boot process appears. This section explores the audible and visual clues that are present during the device's startup, offering an inside look at the workings of the device. Gaining an understanding of the starting sequence helps improve the user-virtual environment interaction.

3.1.3 Advice on Power Management

Maintaining the Vision Pro for an extended period of time requires maximizing battery life and optimizing power utilization. In order to keep your device prepared for your upcoming immersive experience, this section provides advice and best practices for power management. These tips enable users to optimize background operations and screen brightness, thereby maximizing the battery life of their devices.

Section 3.2: Using the Interface

3.2.1 The Digital Dashboard

The primary navigation hub, a virtual dashboard, greets users when they turn on the Vision Pro. This section offers a thorough examination of the dashboard, emphasizing important components including settings, notifications, and app icons.

Users quickly get adept at navigating this interface as they set out on their virtual journeys.

3.2.2 Head Positioning for Guidance

For navigation, the Vision Pro uses cutting-edge head tracking technology. This section describes how little head motions translate into smooth UI navigation. Head tracking is so intuitive that users may explore the virtual world with ease—all they have to do is move their head.

3.2.3 Voice Orders for Easy Management

Voice commands are a potent control technique that the Vision Pro introduces for a fully hands-free experience. With the help of the commands in this section, users may use their voice to open apps, change settings, and carry out a variety of other operations. Voice commands improve the user experience by giving the impression that interacting with the virtual world is fluid.

3.3 Fundamental Motions and Mechanisms

3.3.1 Developing Your Hand Motions

A library of hand gestures that function as the interactional language is introduced by the Vision Pro. This section describes the movements that users can use to interact with virtual items and traverse menus, ranging from pointing to grabbing. Gaining proficiency with these movements generates a sensation of direct interaction with the virtual world and opens up a universe of possibilities.

3.3.2 Integration of Controllers

The Vision Pro is outfitted with a specialized controller for fine control. This section describes the controller's features, including touch-sensitive surfaces and button mappings. Through extensive training, users will learn how to optimize their virtual experiences—whether they are creating, exploring, or gaming—by employing the controller.

3.3.3 Comprehending Haptic Input

The virtual experience gains a tangible component from haptic feedback. This section delves into how the Vision Pro enhances the virtual interaction's feeling of touch by means of the controller, hence providing haptic feedback. Gaining an understanding of the subtleties of haptic feedback makes a virtual reality experience richer in senses and more immersive.

3.4 Modifying the Fit and Straps

3.4.1 Using Adjustable Straps to Ensure Comfort

The fit of the headset has a major impact on how comfortable long VR sessions are. In order to get a tight and secure fit, users can tighten the head straps according to the instructions in this section. Straps that are properly fitted distribute the weight evenly, reducing discomfort and enabling users to enjoy immersive experiences for longer.

3.4.2 Modification of Interpupillary Distance (IPD)

IPD modification makes the visual experience more personalized. In addition to outlining the importance of IPD, this section offers detailed instructions on how to adjust the distance between the lenses to suit each user's individual physiology. Accurate IPD adjustment helps provide crisper images and lessens eye strain while using for extended periods of time.

3.4.3 Compatibility with Prescription Lenses

The Vision Pro accepts customisable prescription lens inserts for users who wear glasses. This section describes how to integrate prescription lenses so that people with different vision needs can experience VR that is both comfortable and crystal clear.

3.4.4 Consistent Upkeep for Extended Life
The lifetime and best performance of the Vision Pro are guaranteed by regular care and maintenance. Practical advice on how to maintain cords, clean the lenses, and store the headset when not in use is provided in this section. Users can protect their device's integrity for countless journeys beyond reality by adopting these techniques into their daily usage.

Users are prepared for the many possibilities that the Apple Vision Pro VR Headset promises as soon as they become adept at turning the headset on and off, navigating the interface with ease, controlling the virtual world with gestures, and making sure it fits comfortably. The experiences and applications that users might expect when they step outside of reality will be covered in detail in the upcoming chapters.

Chapter 4

Examining Particulars

This chapter will act as a guide for you as you learn more about the Apple Vision Pro VR Headset, helping you to explore the many features that contribute to the immersive experience. Discovering amazing virtual worlds, interacting with augmented reality software, adjusting display parameters, and losing yourself in multidimensional audio are just a few of the experiences that await you in each part.

4.1 Virtual Reality Immersions

4.1.1 The Digital Terrain

With the Apple Vision Pro, you may access a variety
of virtual environments that are intended to
stimulate your senses. Users can explore a variety of
well-liked virtual reality experiences in this section,
ranging from calm meditation settings to vibrant
game worlds. Users can explore realistic simulations
with unparalleled realism or meander through
fanciful realms thanks to the immersive trip that
goes beyond the physical.

4.1.2 Beyond Boundaries Gaming

The Vision Pro opens the door to an unmatched
gaming experience for fans of video games. Popular
VR games are included in this section, ranging
from heart-pounding quests to challenging puzzles.
Users will explore the vast and ever-expanding

world of virtual reality games, whether they're taking on opponents in fanciful settings or immersing themselves in realistic sports simulations.

4.1.3 Virtual Expedition and Travel

Virtual travel experiences allow you to explore places beyond geographical bounds. This section walks users through apps that take them to historical sites, exotic locations, and famous landmarks. Take virtual tours that redefine what it means to explore from the comforts of your living room.

4.1.4 Immersion in Education

The Vision Pro is an effective educational tool as well as a portal for enjoyment. The educational VR apps that promote learning through immersive experiences are highlighted in this area. Through immersive experiences such as underwater exploration and space exploration, users can interact with educational content in ways that go beyond conventional approaches.

4.2 Uses for Augmented Reality

4.2.1 Connecting the Virtual and Real Worlds

Applications for augmented reality (AR) enhance daily experiences by bringing the virtual into the real world. Users are introduced to augmented reality (AR) applications in this part, which superimpose digital features on the real world. Users will discover the transformative power of augmented reality through tasks that provide AR assistance and engaging learning experiences.

4.2.2 AR in Creating and Producing

Examine augmented reality applications that transform creativity and productivity. This section explores solutions that let users see 3D models in physical settings, work remotely via augmented reality meetings, and let their creativity run wild with immersive augmented reality art experiences. In the personal and professional domains, augmented reality proves to be a flexible partner.

4.2.3 Using AR to Improve Retail

Shop like never before with augmented reality. This section walks users through AR applications that let them see furniture in real environments, try on clothes virtually, and make well-informed decisions in retail settings. The retail experience is revolutionized by augmented reality, which offers a dynamic and engaging way to shop.

4.2.4 AR in Exploration and Navigation

Utilize augmented reality overlays to navigate the world. Applications that use augmented reality

(AR) for navigation are covered in this section, including those that help you navigate a new city and identify hidden gems around you. Your journey in the real world is perfectly integrated with augmented reality as a navigational tool.

4.3 Customized Display Preferences
4.3.1 Customizing Visual Explicitness

A variety of sophisticated display options are available with the Vision Pro to customize visual clarity to personal tastes. Users can alter brightness, contrast, and color settings with the help of this area. Comprehending these configurations guarantees an individualized visual experience that corresponds with your distinct tastes and amplifies the total immersion.

4.3.2 Field of View Optimization

One of the most important aspects of the immersive experience is the field of view (FOV). This section looks at how users can adjust the field of view (FOV) to balance focus and peripheral vision. Optimizing the field of view enhances the natural and comprehensive virtual reality encounter.

4.3.3 Taking into Account Refresh Rate

In order to maintain visual fluidity, the refresh rate is crucial. The effect of refresh rates on motion clarity and comfort is discussed in this section. By modifying refresh rates according to content and personal tastes, users will be able to optimize the display for a fluid and comfortable viewing experience.

4.3.4 Enhanced Details and Resolution

Gain complete control over the resolution and detail enhancement settings on the Vision Pro display. The details of detail enhancement and resolution modifications are covered in length in this part, giving customers the ability to fine-tune visual quality for an unmatched viewing experience.

4.4 Options for Spatial Audio and Sound

4.4.1 Immersion in 3D Audio

A key component of the immersive experience of the Vision Pro is spatial audio. This section looks at how dynamic soundscapes created with 3D audio technology respond to the user's motions. Spatial audio enhances the auditory aspect of virtual reality in a variety of ways, from directional audio cues in games to immersive music experiences.

4.4.2 Tailoring Audio Preferences

Customize the audio experience with audio settings that you can change to suit your tastes. This section walks users through volume control, balance, and equalization settings. Personalized and ideal auditory experience is ensured by changing audio settings, whether you like a balanced audio profile for movie experiences or deep bass for gaming.

4.4.3 Audio Control using Voice Commands

Use voice commands to expand the hands-free experience to include audio control. This section looks at using voice commands to change tracks, adjust audio settings, and enable particular audio capabilities. Voice-activated audio enhances the immersive experience by providing a convenient layer.

4.4.4 Including External Speakers

The Vision Pro supports external audio devices for those who are audiophiles looking for a high-end audio experience. Step-by-step instructions for connecting and setting up external speakers or headphones are provided in this section. By smoothly integrating premium audio accessories with the Vision Pro, users may enhance their audio experience to new heights.

Users are taking on a voyage that goes beyond reality as they experiment with the immersive VR experiences, interact with augmented reality apps, adjust display settings, and lose themselves in spatial audio. In the following chapters, we'll explore more facets of the Apple Vision Pro VR Headset and walk users through personalization, customisation, and the seemingly endless possibilities that lie beyond reality.

Chapter 5

Apps for Apple Vision Pro

Exploring the diverse ecosystem of applications carefully chosen to enhance your virtual reality experience is the first step towards realizing the full potential of the Apple Vision Pro VR Headset. This chapter will walk you through how to use the App Store, highlight some of the most interesting VR apps, look at productivity and entertainment options, and give you tips on how to keep your app library organized and up to date.

5.1 Using and Accessing the App Store

5.1.1 Easily Navigable App Store

Getting into the App Store is the first step towards exploring the immersive world of the Vision Pro. In this part, users will learn how to easily access the App Store from the headset's UI. Getting around the App Store becomes second nature as you discover the wide range of apps available to you.

5.1.2 Choosing Subjects and Suggested Readings

Explore the carefully picked categories and suggestions in the App Store created just for the Vision Pro. This area offers tips on how to browse and choose apps that suit your interests quickly and effectively, covering everything from productivity and education to gaming and entertainment. Discover well-liked selections and undiscovered treasures that improve your VR experience.

5.1.3 Effortless Application Search and Filters

Simple search and filtering features make it easy to find certain apps. This section explains how to apply filters based on categories, ratings, and user reviews, as well as useful search strategies. Gaining proficiency with these tools will guarantee that you locate the apps that suit your demands and preferences with ease.

5.1.4 Downloading Secure Apps

Security must always come first while trying out new apps. In order to ensure that customers may add programs to their library with confidence and without jeopardizing the integrity of their Vision Pro, this section details the secure download procedure. Because of the App Store's dedication to security and quality, customers have a reliable platform for app exploration.

5.2 VR Showcase Apps

5.2.1 Marvels of Gaming

Enter a world of incredible games created to stretch the limits of virtual reality. The best VR games that make use of the Vision Pro's features are included in this area. From thrilling quests to engrossing simulations, players will find games that completely change the virtual gaming scene.

5.2.2 Immersive Virtual Reality

Enter immersive virtual reality experiences that immerse you in compelling stories and striking visual displays. This section looks at virtual reality stories, documentaries, and movies that make use of the Vision Pro's cutting-edge spatial audio and display technology. Discover new storytelling facets with engaging cinematic material.

5.2.3 Virtual Reality Art Expressions

Use artistic VR applications to unleash the Vision Pro's creative potential. This section explores apps that enable users to express themselves artistically in virtual spaces, ranging from immersive art galleries to virtual painting and sculpting. Discover how creativity and technology can come together in a way that goes beyond conventional creative limitations.

5.2.4 Virtual Reality Health and Fitness
Change your physical health using virtual reality wellness and exercise apps. Apps that provide guided exercise, yoga classes, and wellness experiences designed specifically for the Vision Pro are highlighted in this section. Invest in virtual worlds that are both motivational and entertaining to enhance your workout routine.

5.3 Apps for Entertainment and Productivity

5.3.1 Online Workplace Resource Centers

Virtual suites made for the Vision Pro will usher in a new era of efficiency. Applications for 3D modeling, collaborative workspaces, and virtual meetings are covered in this area. Users will learn how the Vision Pro improves productivity in the virtual world, from professional partnerships to distant work circumstances.

5.3.2 Teaching Virtual Reality Resources

Boost your educational experience with VR resources designed just for Vision Pro users. Applications covering a wide range of educational topics are introduced in this section, including virtual historical tours and interactive science classes. Discover how to use educational VR to study in a way that goes beyond conventional classroom settings and creates a captivating, immersive learning environment.

5.3.3 Entertainment That Isn't Limited

This section features entertainment apps that reimagine live experiences, from virtual concerts to real-world events. Engage in live performances, go to virtual concerts, and take part in activities that connect the virtual and actual worlds. Beyond the bounds of reality, entertainment experiences can be accessed with the Vision Pro.

5.3.4 Virtual Reality Social Environments

Use VR social areas to connect with friends and communities. Applications that provide online meetings, social connections, and cooperative experiences are examined in this section. Users will learn how the Vision Pro changes the way people socialize by establishing shared areas that unite individuals in the virtual world despite geographical barriers.

5.4 App Management and Updates

5.4.1 Consistent Updates for a Smooth Experience
Update your app library automatically to stay
current with ease. In order to guarantee that the
newest features, enhancements, and optimizations
are smoothly incorporated into the Vision Pro
experience, users can enable automatic updates by
following the instructions in this section. Keep up
to date with little effort and enjoy ongoing
improvement.

5.4.2 Version Control and Handled App Updates
There is an option for manual updating for
customers who would like have greater control over
their program updates. This section offers detailed
instructions for managing updates according to
personal preferences, investigating version histories,
and manually updating apps. Organize your app

collection and make sure it fits the experience you want.

5.4.3 App Library Structure

Keeping your app collection organized becomes crucial as it expands. Creating folders, personalizing categories, and ranking your favorite apps are just a few of the tips and tricks covered in this area for effectively organizing your app library. You can easily access the apps that are most important to you with a well-organized library.

5.4.4 Storage Management and App Removal

Optimize your Vision Pro experience by efficiently handling app storage. This section walks users through the process of uninstalling programs, freeing up storage, and improving the speed of the device. Users will gain knowledge on how to properly balance the variety of apps with storage effectiveness.

Exploring the enormous array of Apple Vision Pro apps is a thrilling experience that presents countless opportunities. The Vision Pro transforms into a flexible companion that fits your interests and requirements, whether it is for gaming adventures, educational exploration, entertainment, or productivity boost. The next few chapters will take you farther into the possibilities that are within your reach when you go outside of reality.

Chapter 6

Configuration and Customization

As you delve deeper into the world of the Apple Vision Pro VR Headset, customization turns into the secret to opening up a customized and enhanced virtual reality encounter. This chapter serves as your manual for setting up environments, making unique user profiles, investigating accessibility features, and ensuring that your device is operating at peak efficiency through routine software updates and maintenance.

6.1 Tailoring Settings

6.1.1 Online Environments Customized for You

Customize your virtual reality settings to suit your tastes and emotional state. The customization choices, such as backdrop themes, ambient lighting, and virtual environments, are covered in detail in this section. You may customize your virtual environment with the Vision Pro, choosing from a futuristic or tranquil backdrop.

6.1.2 Building Personalized Environments

Make bespoke surroundings to elevate personalization to a new level. A detailed tutorial on creating and implementing your own virtual places may be found in this section. Users can create their ideal environments by arranging virtual objects and selecting textures, which strengthens their sense of immersion in the virtual world.

6.1.3 Changing Moods and Environments

Investigate dynamic settings that change depending on your activity and mood. Users can learn about features in this section that allow virtual surroundings to be in sync with physical aspects like the weather, the time of day, or even biometric data. The Vision Pro turns into an adaptable canvas that changes as your feelings and experiences do.

6.1.4 Having Others Share Your Environments

Share your personalized surroundings with friends and the Vision Pro community to expand customisation beyond individual encounters. The methods for sharing your works are described in this part, which promotes community building and cooperative innovation in the online environment.

6.2 Character Sets

6.2.1 The Importance of User Profiles A flawless and customized VR experience begins with a user's profile. The importance of user profiles is discussed in this section, with special attention to how they save user preferences, settings, and customized information. Comprehending the function of user profiles establishes the groundwork for a continually customized digital encounter.

6.2.2 Establishing and Taking Care of User Profiles A thorough tutorial on building and maintaining user profiles may be found in this section. In order to guarantee that each person's preferences are upheld and the Vision Pro fluidly adjusts to each user's specific needs, users will learn how to set up multiple profiles for various users or scenarios.

6.2.3 Customized Identifiers and Avatars

Personalize your online persona with unique IDs and avatars. This section explores the avatar modification choices that let users show off their uniqueness in the virtual world. In the context of Vision Pro, avatars become more than just representations of a person's identity—they become extensions of it.

6.2.4 Changing Profiles
Make smooth transitions between user profiles to suit various users or tastes. In order to provide each person with a customized and easy-to-use VR experience, this section walks users through the process of switching between accounts.

6.3 Features for Accessibility
6.3.1 Principles of Inclusive Design
In order to guarantee that the Vision Pro experience is inclusive and suitable for users with a variety of

needs, accessibility features are essential. This section delves into the fundamentals of inclusive design, highlighting Apple's dedication to developing a VR world that is usable by people of different abilities.

6.3.2 Configuring Vision Accessibility
Examine vision accessibility settings designed to accommodate those with visual impairments. An introduction of features including configurable contrast settings, screen reader support, and voice coaching is given in this section. Comprehending and employing these configuration options improves the Vision Pro's usefulness and accessibility for all users.

6.3.3 Options for Hearing Accessibility
Examine hearing accessibility options to ensure that users with hearing problems may participate in the

Vision Pro experience. Features including adjustable audio balance, subtitles, and visual cues for sound occurrences are described in this section. Users are able to customize their audio experience to suit their own hearing requirements.

6.3.4 Cognitive and Motor Accessibility
Users with cognitive and movement impairments can utilize the Vision Pro because of its accessible design. This section presents elements that enable users with varying abilities to travel and interact with the virtual environment, such as voice commands, customized controls, and navigation aids.

6.4 Updating and Maintaining Software
6.4.1 Software Updates' Significance Software updates are essential to preserving the Vision Pro's functionality, security, and performance. The

necessity of routinely upgrading the device's software is emphasized in this section to give users access to the newest improvements, security updates, and bug fixes.

6.4.2 Turning on Automatic Updates Turn on automatic updates to expedite the updating process. Users can make sure their Vision Pro is configured to automatically download and install software updates in the background by following the instructions in this section. Without the need for human intervention, automatic upgrades maintain the device's optimization.

6.4.3 Update Software Manually
Manual updates offer greater flexibility for those who would like have more control over the update process. Step-by-step instructions for manually checking for updates, downloading them, and

installing them whenever it's convenient for you are provided in this section. Users can maintain control over the software development of their devices by doing manual upgrades.

6.4.4 Maintenance and Troubleshooting Advice

Make maintenance and troubleshooting a regular part of your routine to maintain the Vision Pro performing at its best. This section provides helpful advice on how to fix frequent problems, carry out regular maintenance, and make sure the gadget is in good working order for extended periods of time.

You are creating an experience that is perfectly tailored to your tastes and requirements as you work your way through the customisation options, investigate the possibilities of user profiles, take advantage of accessibility features, and keep up with software upgrades and maintenance for the Vision

Pro. The ensuing chapters will take you through social interactions, artistic expression, and the boundless possibilities of virtual reality as you continue to explore the enormous potential of the Apple Vision Pro VR Headset.

Chapter 7

Troubleshooting and FAQs

Embarking on the immersive journey with the Apple Vision Pro VR Headset is an exhilarating experience, but as with any technological marvel, occasional challenges may arise. This chapter serves as your comprehensive guide to troubleshooting common issues, accessing customer support channels, and addressing frequently asked questions to ensure a seamless and enjoyable experience with your Vision Pro.

7.1 Common Issues and Solutions

7.1.1 Headset Power and Connectivity

Issue 1: The headset doesn't power on.

Solution: Ensure that the battery is charged and the power button is pressed and held until the startup sequence initiates. If the issue persists, check the charging cable, power adapter, and try a different power source.

Issue 2: Connectivity issues with devices.

Solution: Restart the headset and the connected device. Check for software updates on both the headset and the connected device. Verify that Bluetooth or other connectivity options are enabled and try pairing the devices again.

7.1.2 Display and Visual Quality

Issue 3: Blurry or distorted visuals.

Solution: Adjust the head straps for a secure fit, and ensure that the lenses are clean. Check the display settings for resolution and detail enhancements. If the issue persists, restart the headset and recalibrate the sensors.

Issue 4: Screen freezing or flickering.
Solution: Restart the headset to refresh the display. If the issue persists, check for software updates. If using external devices, ensure their compatibility and try connecting them again. If the problem continues, contact customer support.

7.1.3 Audio and Spatial Sound
Issue 5: No audio or spatial sound.
Solution: Check the audio settings to ensure the volume is not muted. If using external audio devices, ensure they are properly connected. If the issue persists, restart the headset, and check for

software updates. If spatial audio is still not working, contact customer support.

Issue 6: Audio lag or delay.
Solution: Ensure that all connected devices have the latest firmware and software updates. Check for interference from other wireless devices and try adjusting the audio settings. If the problem persists, contact customer support for further assistance.

7.1.4 Controls and Interactions
Issue 7: Controller not responding.
Solution: Ensure the controller is charged. Restart the headset and repair the controller if necessary. If the issue persists, check for software updates and, if needed, contact customer support for further assistance.

Issue 8: Hand gestures not recognized.

Solution: Ensure proper lighting conditions for hand tracking. Check for obstructions or reflections that may interfere with sensors. If the problem persists, recalibrate hand tracking in the settings menu.

7.2 Customer Support Channels

7.2.1 Online Support Resources

Apple provides extensive online support resources for Vision Pro users. Visit the official Apple Support website for troubleshooting guides, user manuals, and FAQs. The online support resources are regularly updated, providing users with a wealth of information to address common issues independently.

7.2.2 Live Chat and Email Support

Engage with Apple's customer support team through live chat or email. The live chat option allows users to connect with support representatives in real-time, receiving personalized assistance for specific issues. Email support provides a written record of communication, ensuring thorough and detailed responses to user queries.

7.2.3 Phone Support

For immediate assistance, users can contact Apple's phone support. The dedicated support hotline connects users with knowledgeable representatives who can guide them through troubleshooting steps or provide information on warranty and repair services. Phone support is especially useful for complex issues that may require real-time interaction.

7.2.4 In-Person Support at Apple Stores

Visit an Apple Store for in-person support and assistance. Apple's retail locations offer hands-on support through the Genius Bar. Schedule an appointment or walk in for personalized assistance from Apple's technical experts. In-person support is beneficial for issues that require physical examination or hands-on troubleshooting.

7.3 Frequently Asked Questions

7.3.1 General Queries

Q1: How do I clean the lenses of the Vision Pro?

A1: Use a microfiber cloth to gently clean the lenses. Avoid using harsh cleaning agents or abrasive materials that may damage the lenses. Refer to the user manual for detailed cleaning instructions.

Q2: Can I wear glasses with the Vision Pro?

A2: Yes, the Vision Pro accommodates users who wear prescription glasses. Additionally, customizable prescription lens inserts are available for users with varying visual needs.

7.3.2 Connectivity and Compatibility

Q3: Can I connect the Vision Pro to non-Apple devices?

A3: The Vision Pro is designed for seamless integration with Apple devices, ensuring optimal performance and compatibility. While some features may be limited on non-Apple devices, certain connectivity options are available.

Q4: Is the Vision Pro compatible with third-party VR applications?

A4: The Vision Pro is optimized for the Apple ecosystem, and compatibility with third-party VR applications may vary. Check the App Store for supported applications and updates.

7.3.3 Battery and Power Management

Q5: How long does the battery of the Vision Pro last?

A5: Battery life depends on usage patterns. On average, the Vision Pro offers several hours of continuous use on a single charge. For extended use, consider adjusting display settings to optimize battery performance.

Q6: Can I use the Vision Pro while it's charging?

A6: Yes, the Vision Pro can be used while charging. However, prolonged use while charging may impact battery longevity over time.

7.3.4 Software and Updates

Q7: How do I check for software updates on the Vision Pro?

A7: Navigate to the settings menu, select "Software Update," and follow the on-screen instructions to check for and install the latest updates.

Q8: Can I roll back to a previous software version?
A8: Apple typically does not support rolling back to previous software versions. It is recommended to keep the device updated to ensure access to the latest features, improvements, and security patches.

Troubleshooting and FAQs are valuable resources for ensuring a smooth and enjoyable experience with the Apple Vision Pro VR Headset. Whether addressing common issues, seeking assistance from customer support channels, or exploring frequently asked questions, users can navigate challenges with confidence, ensuring that their journey beyond reality remains immersive and trouble-free.

Chapter 8

Future Developments

As technology continues its relentless march forward, the landscape of virtual reality is poised for continuous evolution, and the Apple Vision Pro VR Headset stands at the forefront of this dynamic journey. In this chapter, we explore the exciting prospects of the future, delving into Apple's Vision Pro roadmap, anticipating upcoming features and enhancements, and valuing the input of the community through feedback and suggestions.

8.1 Apple's Vision Pro Roadmap

8.1.1 Vision Pro as a Platform

Apple envisions the Vision Pro not just as a device but as a comprehensive platform for immersive experiences. The roadmap underscores Apple's commitment to expanding the ecosystem around the Vision Pro, fostering an environment where developers can innovate and users can explore a diverse range of applications, content, and services.

8.1.2 Integration with Apple Ecosystem

The future development of the Vision Pro aligns closely with the broader Apple ecosystem. Seamless integration with other Apple devices, services, and platforms is a key focus. This integration aims to enhance user convenience, allowing for effortless transitions between the Vision Pro and other Apple products.

8.1.3 Collaborations and Partnerships

Anticipate collaborations and partnerships that will bring new dimensions to the Vision Pro experience. Apple is expected to engage with content creators, developers, and industry partners to deliver exclusive content, applications, and features that leverage the full potential of the Vision Pro's capabilities.

8.1.4 Accessibility Advancements

Apple remains dedicated to making technology accessible to all users. The Vision Pro's roadmap includes advancements in accessibility features, ensuring that the device continues to cater to users with diverse abilities. This includes refining existing features and introducing new tools that enhance inclusivity within the virtual realm.

8.2 Upcoming Features and Enhancements

8.2.1 Enhanced Display Technology

The future of the Vision Pro promises advancements in display technology. Expect higher resolutions, improved refresh rates, and enhanced color reproduction. These developments aim to elevate visual fidelity, providing users with an even more immersive and lifelike experience within the virtual environment.

8.2.2 Expanded Gesture and Control Options

Apple is exploring expanded gesture and control options to further enhance user interactions. Future updates may introduce new hand gestures, controller functionalities, and innovative ways to navigate and manipulate virtual content. The goal is to make interactions more intuitive and responsive.

8.2.3 Artificial Intelligence Integration

The integration of artificial intelligence (AI) is on the horizon for the Vision Pro. AI algorithms could play a role in personalizing content recommendations, optimizing virtual environments based on user preferences, and even enhancing the realism of virtual simulations through intelligent adaptation.

8.2.4 Augmented Reality Fusion

While the Vision Pro primarily focuses on virtual reality, Apple is exploring ways to seamlessly integrate augmented reality (AR) elements into the experience. This fusion of VR and AR could open up new possibilities, allowing users to interact with virtual content in the context of the real world.

8.3 Community Feedback and Suggestions
8.3.1 User Feedback Integration

User feedback is a valuable resource in shaping the future of the Vision Pro. Apple is committed to actively listening to user experiences, concerns, and suggestions. Future updates and developments will likely incorporate insights gathered from the Vision Pro community to address common issues and enhance overall user satisfaction.

8.3.2 Community-Driven Content Creation
Apple recognizes the creative potential within the Vision Pro community. The roadmap includes initiatives to empower users to contribute to the platform through community-driven content creation. This may involve tools and features that enable users to share and collaborate on virtual experiences, enriching the collective Vision Pro ecosystem.

8.3.3 Open Development Environment

The Vision Pro's future development aims to create a more open and collaborative environment for developers. Apple is exploring ways to provide developers with greater flexibility, access to advanced tools, and opportunities to contribute to the growth of the Vision Pro platform. This approach encourages a vibrant developer community and a diverse range of applications.

8.3.4 Regular Software Updates

Expect regular software updates to keep the Vision Pro at the forefront of technological advancements. Apple's commitment to continuous improvement means that users can anticipate a stream of updates, introducing new features, optimizations, and enhancements that contribute to the device's longevity and relevance.

As we peer into the future of the Apple Vision Pro VR Headset, the roadmap unveils a thrilling trajectory of innovation and expansion. From the integration with the broader Apple ecosystem to advancements in display technology, expanded control options, AI integration, and the fusion of augmented reality, the Vision Pro promises to be a dynamic and evolving platform.

The input of the Vision Pro community, your insights, feedback, and suggestions, will play a pivotal role in shaping this future. As we collectively journey beyond reality, the Apple Vision Pro stands as a testament to the boundless potential of immersive technology, with an exciting horizon that invites exploration, collaboration, and the continuous pursuit of new frontiers.

Chapter 9

Wrap-Up

Now that we've completed this immersive journey through the Apple Vision Pro VR Headset manual, it's time to take stock of the amazing features, offer closing thoughts and suggestions, and offer sincere gratitude to everyone who helped bring this ground-breaking device to life.

9.1 Summary of Main Elements

9.1.1 Magnificent Exhibition and Visual Encounter

The impressive display and visual capabilities of the Vision Pro serve as the foundation for its main features. Users are taken to virtual worlds with never-before-seen realism thanks to high resolutions, brilliant colors, and improved clarity. When it comes to immersive visual experiences, the gadget's display technology raises the bar for anything from gaming to instructional simulations to virtual landscape exploration.

9.1.2 Virtual Reality Sound Design

A key component of the Vision Pro experience is spatial audio, which gives users a dynamic auditory dimension that changes with their movements. The Vision Pro makes sure that the auditory experience is just as fascinating as the visual one, with configurable audio settings and 3D audio immersion in virtual surroundings.

9.1.3 Natural Controls and Arrangements

With the controls and interactions of the Vision Pro, navigating the virtual world is easy and intuitive. Users can precisely handle virtual items through the use of hand controllers or hand tracking technologies, creating new opportunities for artistic expression, productivity, and immersive gaming experiences.

9.1.4 User profiles and personalization

The Vision Pro transforms from a gadget into a customized extension of the user. Adaptable settings, changing backdrops, and user accounts guarantee that the digital realm corresponds with personal tastes. Each user's distinct identity is accommodated by the Vision Pro, which can create individualized avatars and distinctive locations.

9.1.5 Sturdy Networking Throughout the Apple Ecosystem

The Vision Pro's smooth integration with the larger Apple ecosystem sets it apart as a flexible and networked gadget. The Vision Pro and other Apple products may be switched between with ease, giving users a seamless and cohesive experience across the Apple ecosystem.

9.1.6 Forward-Looking Ideas

The Vision Pro roadmap looks forward to some interesting new innovations. With the ability to integrate artificial intelligence and combine augmented reality with improved display technologies and more control options, the Vision

Pro is ready to keep up with the latest advancements in technology.

9.2 Concluding Remarks and Advice

9.2.1 Beyond Actuality: A Change in Perspective

The way we view and use technology has changed dramatically with the release of the Apple Vision Pro VR Headset. It invites users to explore, create, learn, and connect within realistic virtual settings, pushing the boundaries of reality. The Vision Pro is more than just a tool; it's a doorway to endless opportunities.

9.2.2 Customizing the Online Experience

Users are empowered to customize their virtual experiences thanks to the emphasis on personalization and user profiles. With features like avatar creation and virtual environment customization, the Vision Pro makes sure that every user's experience is distinct and represents their tastes. One factor contributing to the device's unmatched user-centric design is the capacity to customize and curate the virtual environment.

9.2.3 A Future of Collaboration

Future advancements of the Vision Pro will focus on community interaction and teamwork. A collaborative future is indicated by Apple's dedication to incorporating community-driven content production, promoting open development environments, and paying attention to user feedback. Users actively participate in the development of the Vision Pro platform, not only as consumers.

9.2.4 Suggestions for the Best Possible Experience

A few suggestions can improve users' overall experience as they begin their Vision Pro journey:

Keep Up with: To gain access to security patches, new features, and improvements, regularly check for software updates.

Examine a Variety of Content: Explore the wide range of apps that are available on the App Store. The Vision Pro provides a wide range of opportunities to explore, from productivity and education to gaming and enjoyment.

Establish Communication and Cooperation: Use the social areas and teamwork tools on the Vision Pro to establish virtual connections with friends, groups, and other fans.

Give and Receive: As the Vision Pro community expands, think about uploading your works, offering criticism, and actively engaging in the cooperative atmosphere that characterizes the site.

9.3 Recognitions

The development of the Apple Vision Pro VR Headset is a team effort including the commitment and knowledge of many people. We sincerely thank the following:

The Apple Development Team: For their unwavering dedication to innovation, pushing the envelope in virtual reality, and creating an intriguing gadget.

The Vision Pro experience has been improved for all users thanks to the invaluable feedback and practical use of beta testers and early adopters.

Vision Pro Community: For the shared zeal, imagination, and passion among members of the community. Your participation, comments, and input are what drive the Vision Pro platform.

To sum up, the Apple Vision Pro VR Headset is more than just a gadget—it's a call to explore the unusual and venture outside of reality into a world where the limits of the imagination are unlocked. I wish you an endless amount of experiences, unbounded creativity, and an incredibly memorable virtual world connection as you start your Vision Pro journey.

We are grateful that you have opted for the Apple Vision Pro VR Headset, where you may now live remarkable experiences.

www.ingramcontent.com/pod-product-compliance
Lightning Source LLC
LaVergne TN
LVHW051716050326
832903LV00032B/4232